# SHADOWGRAPHS
## Anyone can make

This book, created and drawn by Phila H. Webb with verses by Jane Corby, is reprinted and adapted from the original edition, first published in 1927. Printed in the United States. All rights reserved under the Pan-American and International Copyright Conventions. Originally published by Stoll & Edwards Co., Inc., New York. This book may not be reproduced in whole or in part in any form or by any means, electronic or mechanical, including photocopying, recording, or by any information storage and retrieval system now known or hereafter invented, without written permission from the publisher.

9  8  7  5
Digit on the right indicates the number of this printing.

Library of Congress Cataloging-in-Publication Number 90-50896, ISBN 1-56138-014-8. This book may be ordered by mail from the publisher. Please add $2.50 for postage and handling. *But try your bookstore first!* Running Press, 125 South Twenty-second Street, Philadelphia, Pennsylvania 19103.

## RUNNING PRESS
### PHILADELPHIA · LONDON

# THE FIRST MOVING PICTURES

SHADOW PICTURES were really the first moving pictures. Little boys and girls have been enjoying them for—oh, years and years! Ever since the first grandmother discovered that the shadow of her hand on the wall looked like a swan's head, or perhaps some child first made the great discovery; but at any rate it was long ago. Ever since then people have been thinking of new ways of holding their fingers to get different shadows, so that now there is a long list of animals and objects that can be brought to life in shadow pictures.

The great advantage of the shadow kind of "movies" lies in the fact that nothing is needed except a light and a flat, light-colored surface; these are to be found in every home. The stronger the light and the whiter the flat surface, the clearer the shadow picture will be. A sheet tacked against the wall or thrown over a door makes the finest screen in the world and the ordinary electric bulb makes the right kind of light. If the rest of the room can be darkened as much as possible, the shadow picture on the screen will show up much clearer by contrast.

Pictures of different sizes are obtained by holding the hands nearer the light, or farther from it. All of the pictures in this book can be made by children. A little practice is required in some of the more difficult poses but there is nothing hard about any of them. Probably, in trying to get these pictures, the little shadow-makers will accidentally invent new poses of their own. That's part of the fun of shadow pictures—no one ever quite knows what is going to appear on the screen!

Jane Corby.

RIGHT

LEFT

# OLD MOTHER HUBBARD

Here's the old woman whose troubles were many,
Who looked for a bone when she didn't have any.
No matter; she made shadow pictures instead
For her dog—he forgot that he hadn't been fed!

**Suggestions:** By moving the two middle fingers of your left hand, after you have them in position, you can make Mother Hubbard appear to be talking. Or by moving your little finger a tiny bit, you can make her chin wobble in a funny way.

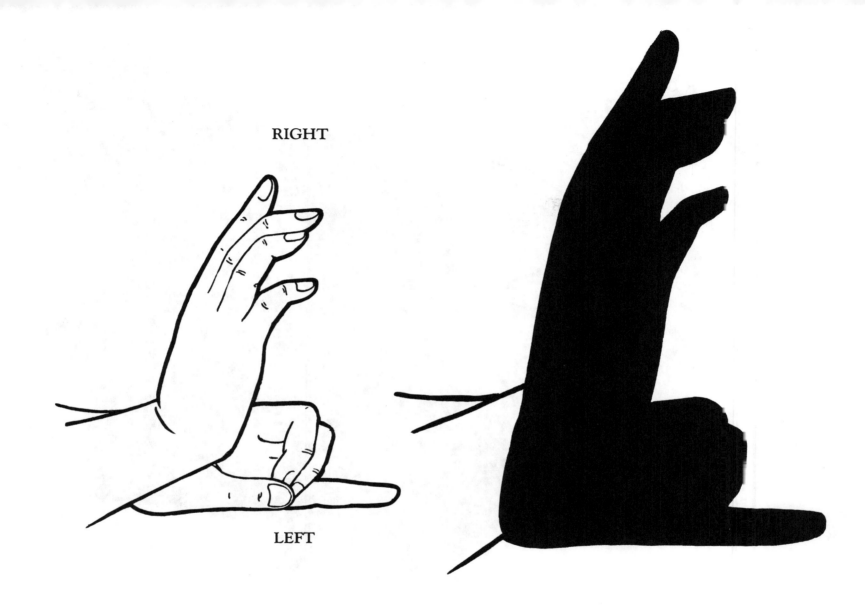

RIGHT

LEFT

# MOTHER HUBBARD'S DOG

This is her dog; he is begging, you see,
For more shadow pictures—how clever is he!
He can wriggle his ears to express his delight,
And wag his tail, too, if you're making him right.

**Suggestions:** This delighted dog, who appears to be smiling, can be made to look as if he were barking, if you move the two middle fingers of the right hand, keeping them together, and move the little finger at the same time. Wag his tail by wagging the thumb of the left hand and wriggle his ears by wriggling the forefinger of your right hand.

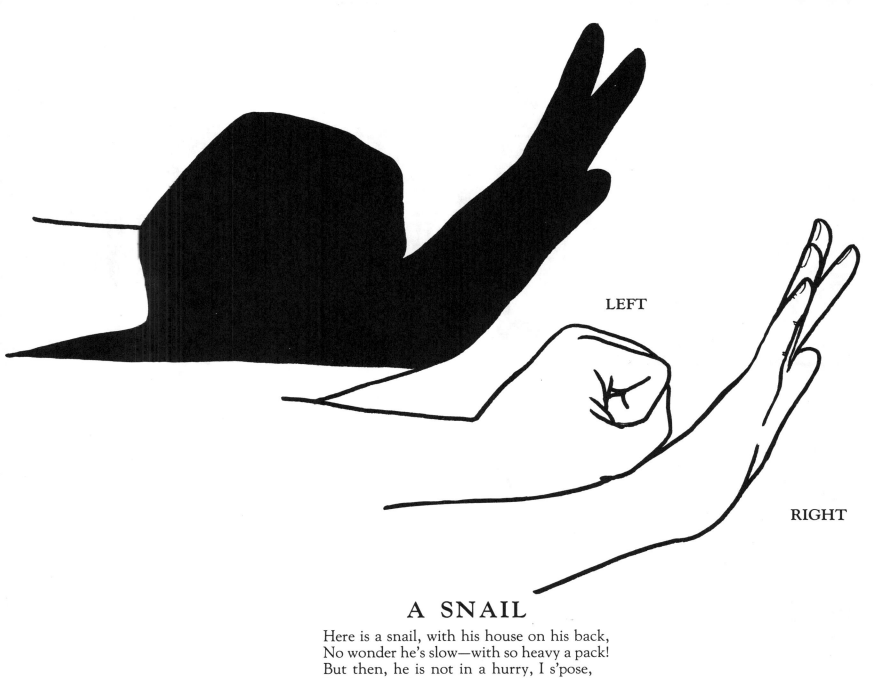

LEFT

RIGHT

## A SNAIL

Here is a snail, with his house on his back,
No wonder he's slow—with so heavy a pack!
But then, he is not in a hurry, I s'pose,
For he is at home, wherever he goes!

**Suggestions:** Move both hands, very slowly, forward and the snail will appear to be on his way. Move the whole left hand a little, from side to side, to make the house sway as he goes. Every once in a while stop and bend the fingers of the right hand forward and backward, as if Mr. Snail were tossing his little horns.

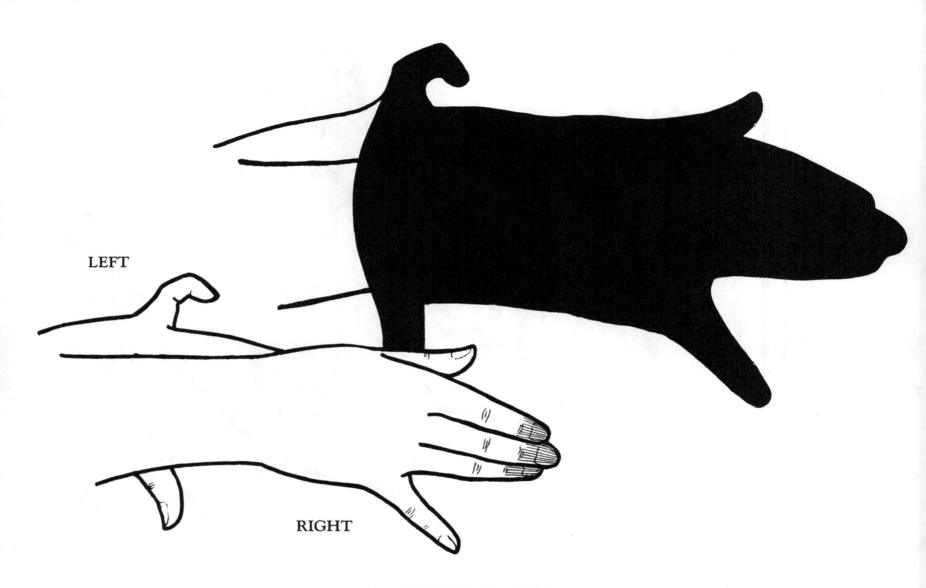

LEFT

RIGHT

## A LITTLE PIG

This little pig went to market and bought
All the things he was sent for, as little pigs ought.
And he didn't cry, "Wee!", but like a good pig,
He hurried home happily, jig-a-jig-jig!

**Suggestions:** The little pig's curly tail will curl and uncurl very nicely if you curl and uncurl the little finger on your left hand. Making him jig is harder but you can do it if you can move the little finger of your right hand and the thumb of your left at the same time.

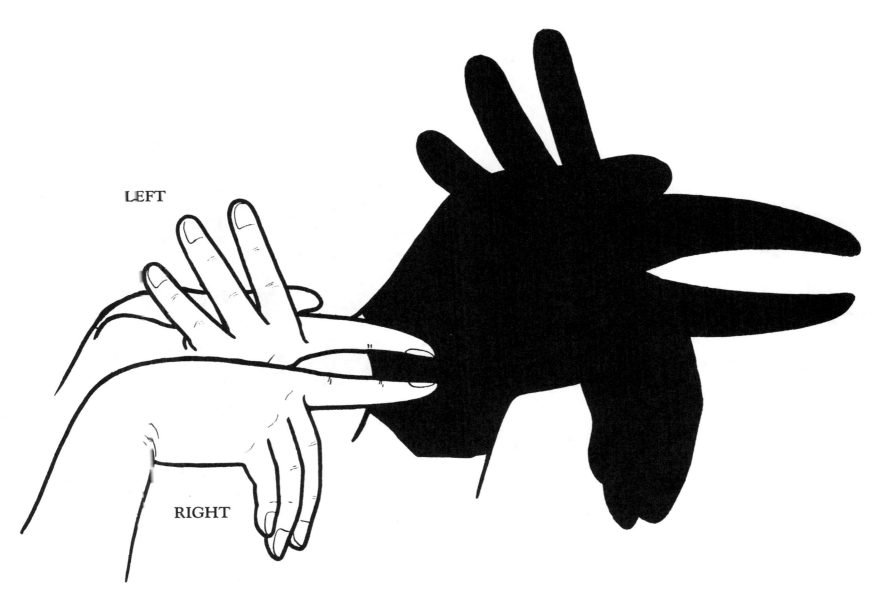

LEFT

RIGHT

# THE CROWING COCK

This is the cock that crowed in the morn
Because he wanted a breakfast of corn;
He woke the farmer, bent with age—
You'll find him on opposite page.

**Suggestions:** This looks a great deal harder than it is but if you get the left hand into position first you will see that it is easy to manage the right one. Show how the cock crows by opening and shutting the two forefingers that form the beak.

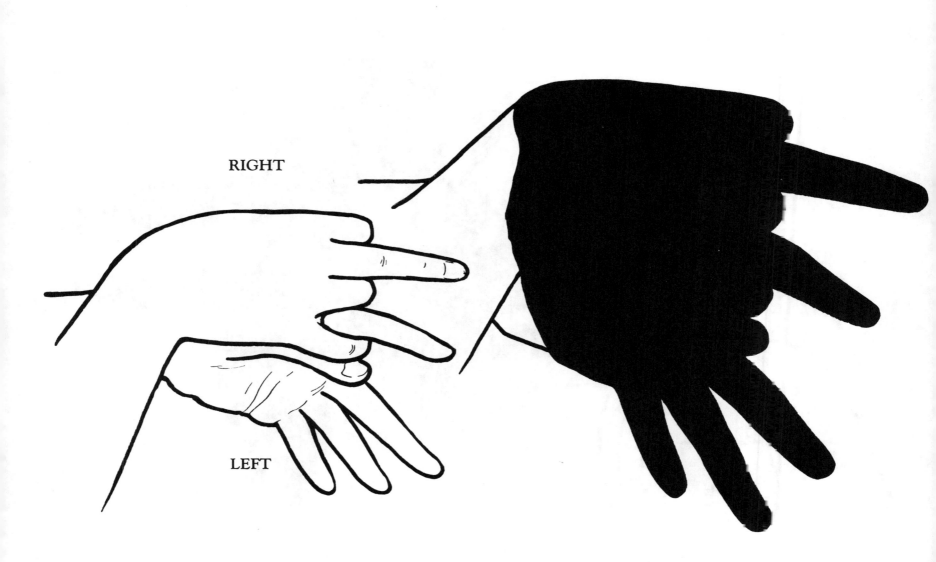

RIGHT

LEFT

# THE FARMER IN THE DELL

Here is the Farmer in the Dell
Who took a wife—you know him well.
Heigh-ho! The farmers only know
How oats and beans and barley grow.

**Suggestions:** Notice that the farmer's nose is the forefinger of the left hand caught between the little finger and the third finger of the right hand. His whiskers will wag if you move the last three fingers on your left hand.

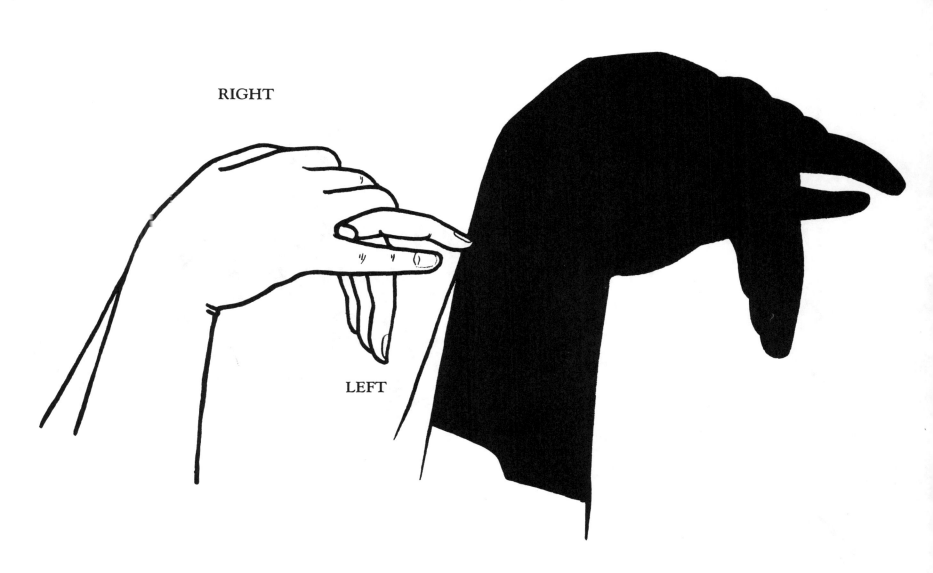

# TURKEY IN THE HAY

This is turkey in the hay,
Who gobbles all the livelong day;
You cannot catch him if you try,
For he can run and he can fly.

**Suggestions:** When you have made the turkey gobble, by moving the forefinger of your left hand up and down against the little finger of your right hand, you ought to move the three fingers of the left hand that form the turkey's wattles, because when a turkey gobbles his wattles shake, of course.

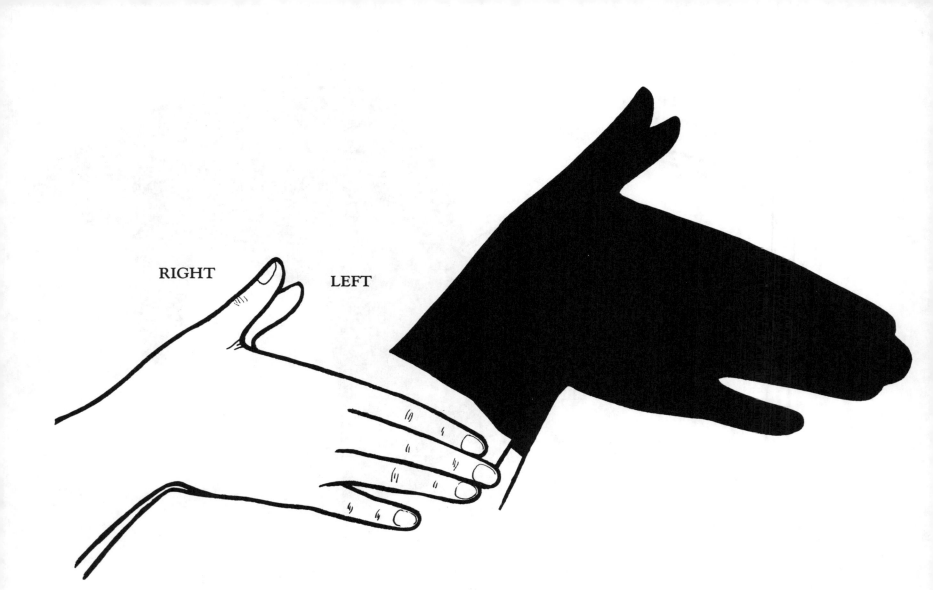

RIGHT    LEFT

# DAPPLE GRAY

Here is the pony, whose name is Dapple Gray,
Once borrowed by a lady to ride a mile away;
She whipped him and she lashed him—oh, how could she do that?
He's such a knowing pony he only needs a pat.

**Suggestions:** You can make Dapple Gray go anywhere you like, forwards or backwards, by moving your hands along the screen. Raise and lower your two hands, held in position, as you move them along and Dapple Gray will appear to be galloping.

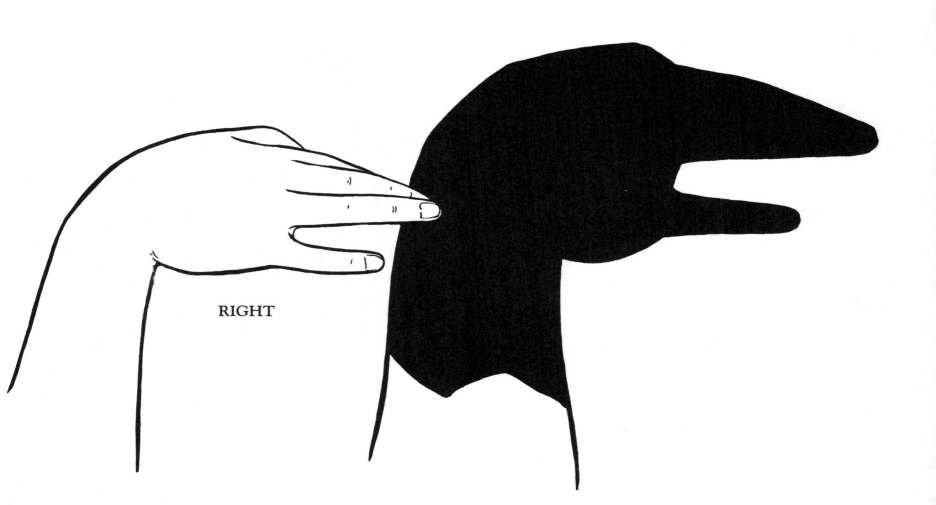

RIGHT

# GOOSEY, GOOSEY, GANDER

This is old Goosey, who wandered about,
Upstairs and downstairs, indoors and out;
Goosey, Goosey, Gander likes to strut around
To see if any stray corn is lying on the ground.

**Suggestions:** Open and shut Goosey's beak by moving your fingers and every now and then dip your hands, hold together, downward sharply, as if Goosey had stopped for a kernel of corn.

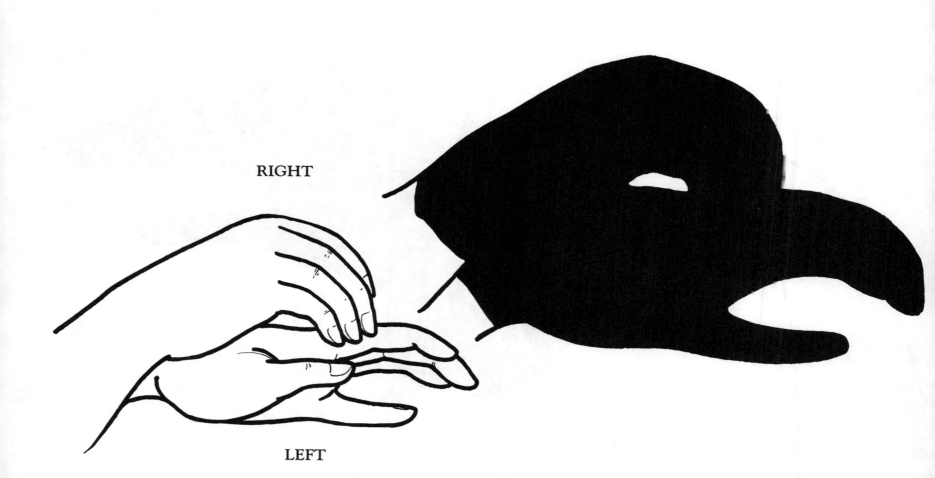

RIGHT

LEFT

# POLLY WANTS A CRACKER!

Here is the Polly of whom you've heard tell,
She wants a nice cracker—you know the words well.
Nice Polly—so pretty!  A cracker she'll get,
Though we haven't got one to give to her yet.

**Suggestions:** Warn your audience to keep away from Polly's dangerous-looking beak.  You can show how she would eat a cracker, if she had one, by bringing the three fingers of the left hand down upon the little finger, letting the upper beak protrude a little, as a polly's does.  An assistant can put a cracker in Polly's mouth, if you like.

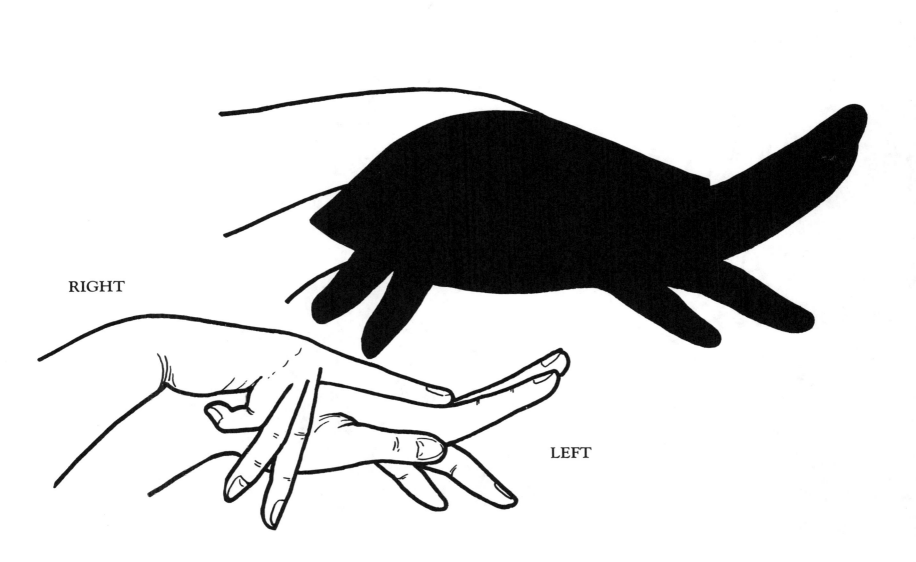

RIGHT

LEFT

# A TORTOISE

This is the tortoise who once won a race,
By going at no very furious pace;
He beat a swift rabbit, but only because
He kept going always, without any pause.

**Suggestions:** Perseverance, you see, always wins. Keep trying and you'll make as good-looking a tortoise as we have on this page.  Move the two first fingers on your left hand, very slowly, from side to side, the way a tortoise does.

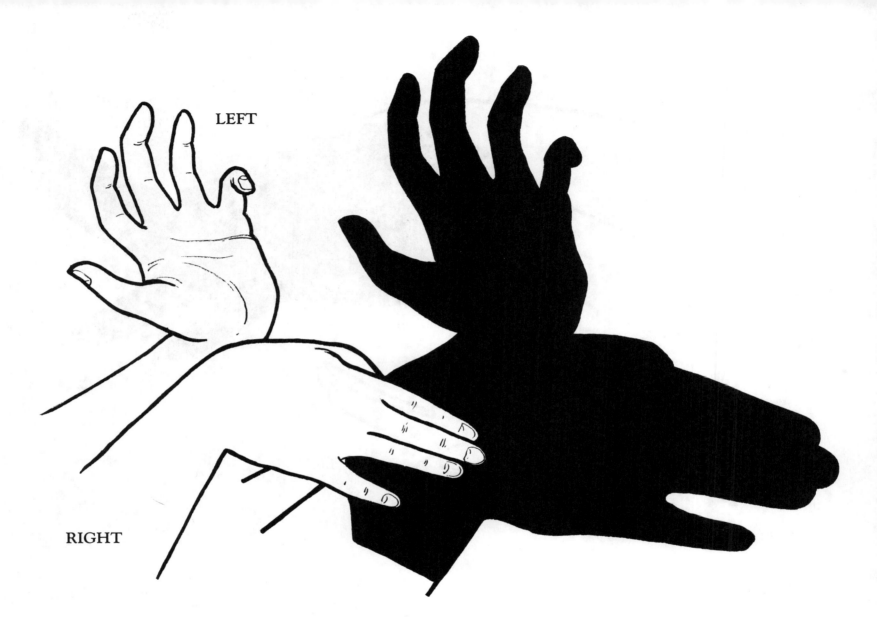

LEFT

RIGHT

# A MOOSE

This is a moose, who roams the wild wood;
He does not care for cities—indeed no moose could.
A moose in a city must live in a zoo;
I am glad that I've made a wild moose, aren't you?

**Suggestions:** Moose are in the habit of tossing their heads from time to time. Toss your hands, up and backward a little, without changing their position, to get a moose-like effect.

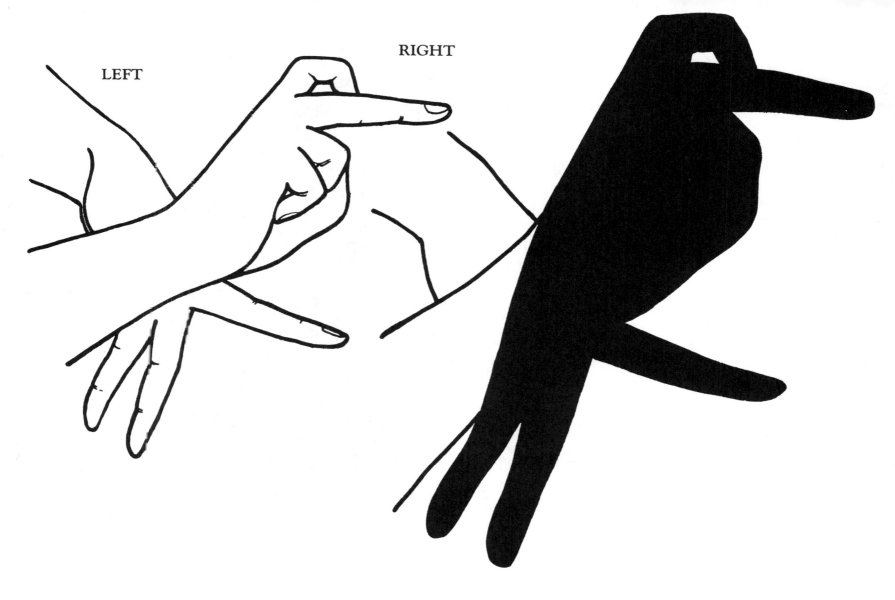

LEFT

RIGHT

# A WOODPECKER

This smart little bird is a doctor of trees;
Our woods would soon die without doctors like these.
Peck! Peck! Not a bug can escape his keen sight;
Now you watch as sharply and get this bird right.

**Suggestions:** Move the hands forward quickly, and back again, as if the woodpecker were darting at an insect. The forefinger of the left hand, extended, gives the perch. The thumb of the left hand, clasping the little finger of the same hand, keeps both out of sight.

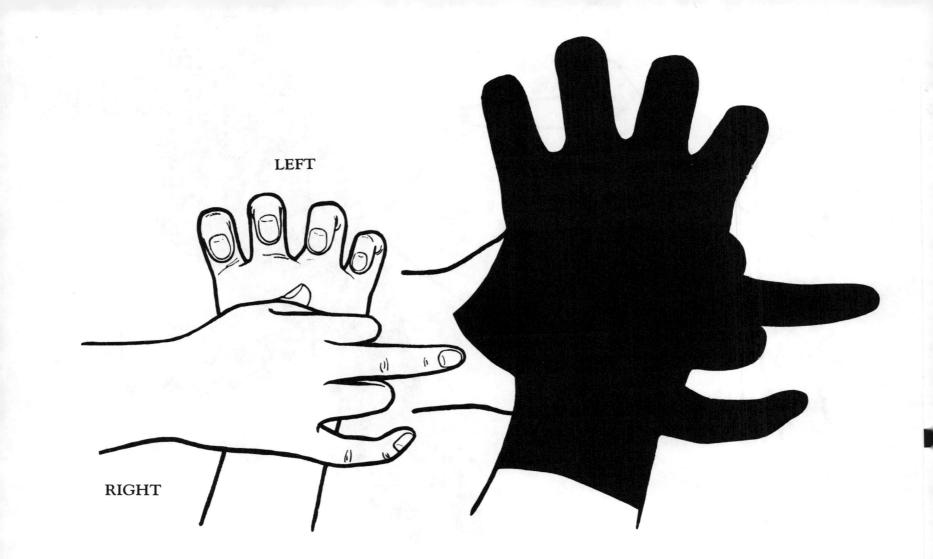

LEFT

RIGHT

## OLD KING COLE

Here is Old King Cole—the merry old soul!
He wears his crown on the top of his head,
Perhaps he is waiting for his pipe and bowl.
And is always merry, as I have said.

**Suggestions:** Old King Cole is pretty easy to make. If you have a pipe handy, you can let him hold it in his mouth—letting the little finger of the right hand keep it in place against the wrist of the left hand.

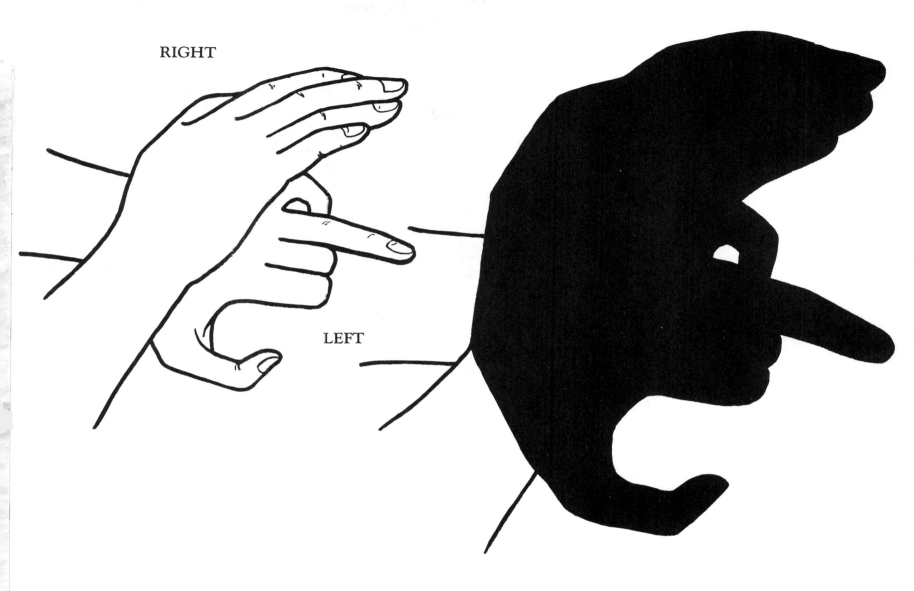

RIGHT

LEFT

# THE COURT JESTER

This jester looks quite solemn, but clowns are apt to be;
Their business is to make us laugh, not laugh themselves, you see.
It's funny just to see him, but when he shows his tricks,
And wig-wags with his long nose, you'll laugh enough for six.

**Suggestions:** The third finger of the left hand, which forms the jester's nose, can be wriggled to make him look funnier. You can make his cap bob, too, by moving the whole right hand without changing the fingers.

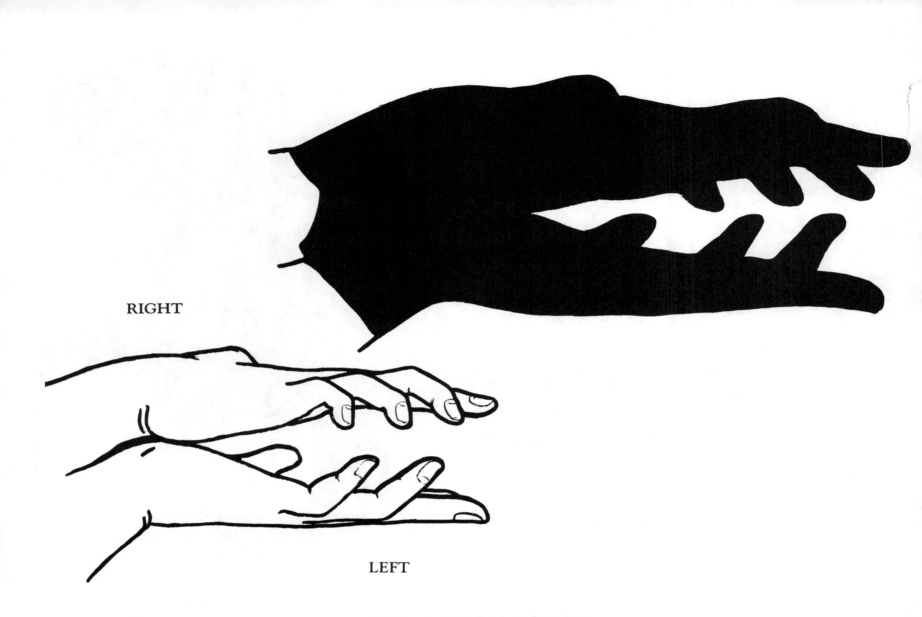

RIGHT

LEFT

# AN ALLIGATOR

This is a 'gator; How well he must bite
With all those long teeth that are out in plain sight!
I hope that no 'gator comes snapping round me,
For they are quite dangerous as I can see.

**Suggestions:** Move the two hands, without disturbing the fingers, together and apart again quickly, so that the alligator's jaws will snap. At the same time move forward along the screen, as if the creature were travelling at a rapid rate.

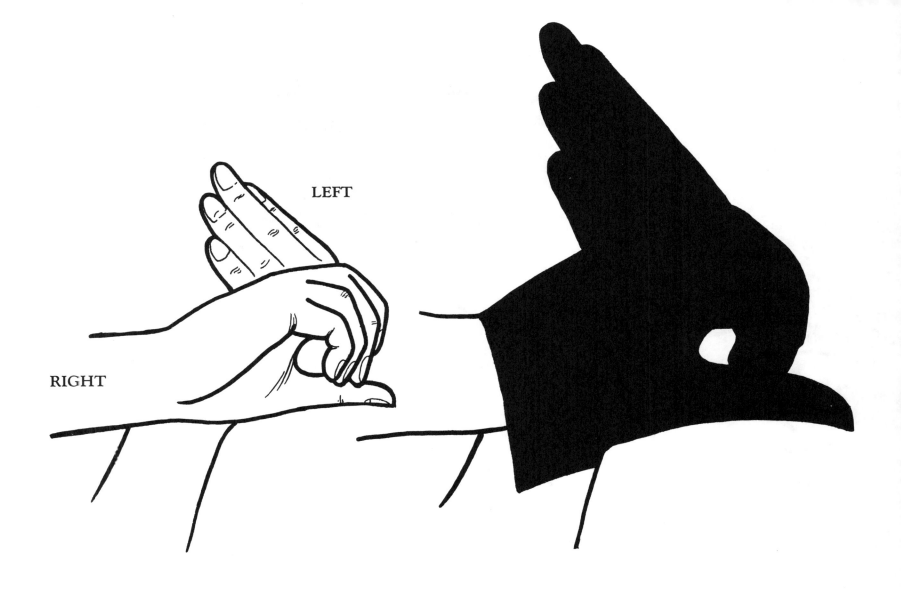

LEFT

RIGHT

## A COCKATOO

Here's a very fine bird—the gay cockatoo!
A lot of good tricks this birdie can do.
He can bow when you tell him and wave his fine crest;
Oh, he is an actor that ranks with the best!

**Suggestions:** Bend both hands forward to make the cockatoo bow and wave the fingers of the left hand to make him wave his crest. The thumb of the right hand, when bent upward and straightened quickly, makes the bird appear to be eating.

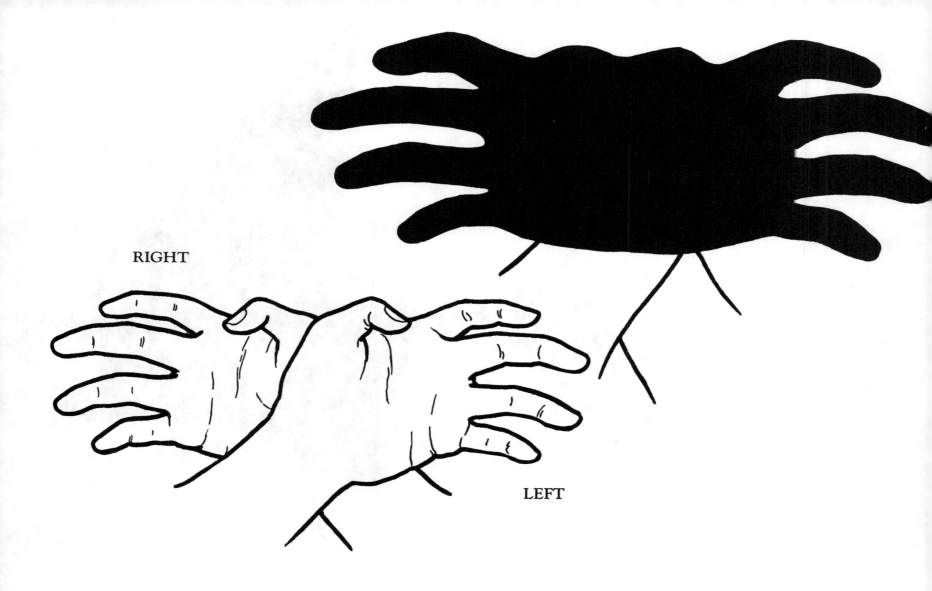

RIGHT

LEFT

# A CRAB

This crab is alive for he's never been caught,
He runs from all danger as every crab ought.
He has many fine legs and they help him run fast;
Just watch and you'll see him go scurrying past.

**Suggestions:** Move all the fingers on both hands as you go forward along the screen. Remember that a crab goes a little sideways, not straight ahead.

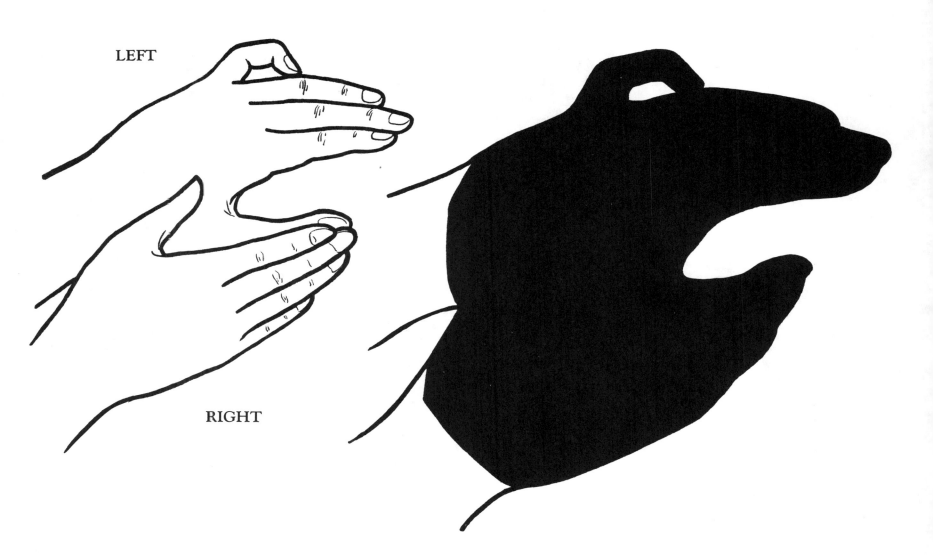

LEFT

RIGHT

## A FROG

This is the frog who would, you know,
Across the field a-wooing go.
He went to woo Miss Mouse, they tell,
Of this frog who lived in a well.

**Suggestions:** Move the whole right hand, gently, and you will see the frog's throat throbbing in a lifelike manner.

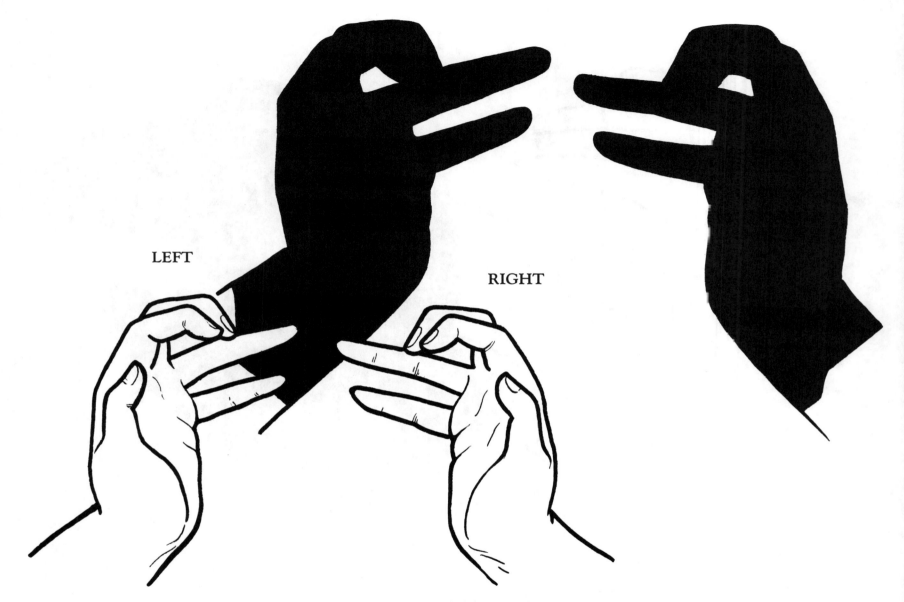

LEFT

RIGHT

## TWO BABY BIRDS

These baby birds go rockaby,
In their tree-top nest when the breezes sigh.
Rockaby baby, in the tree-top,
When the wind doesn't blow, the cradle will stop.

**Suggestions:** Make the baby birds open and shut their mouths by opening and shutting the fingers. Let the hands sway as if the birds were being rocked in their nest.

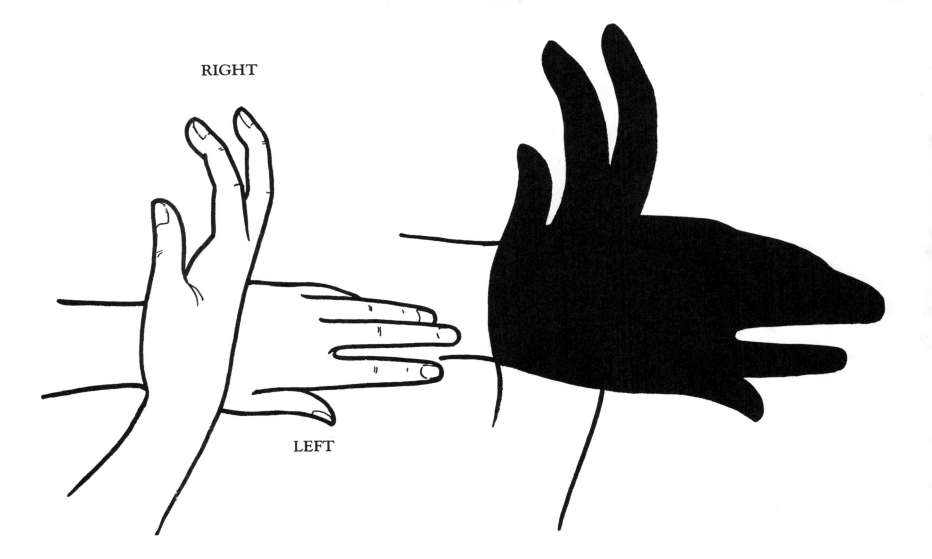

RIGHT

LEFT

## A BILLY-GOAT

Here's old Billy Goat, with a beard on his chin;
You can't keep him out for he'll butt his way in.
He will butt his way through a fence or a door,
Eat all that's in sight and go hunting for more.

**Suggestions:** Billy Goat is not expected to do more than waggle his beard. The thumb of the left hand, which forms the beard, can waggle easily in this position.

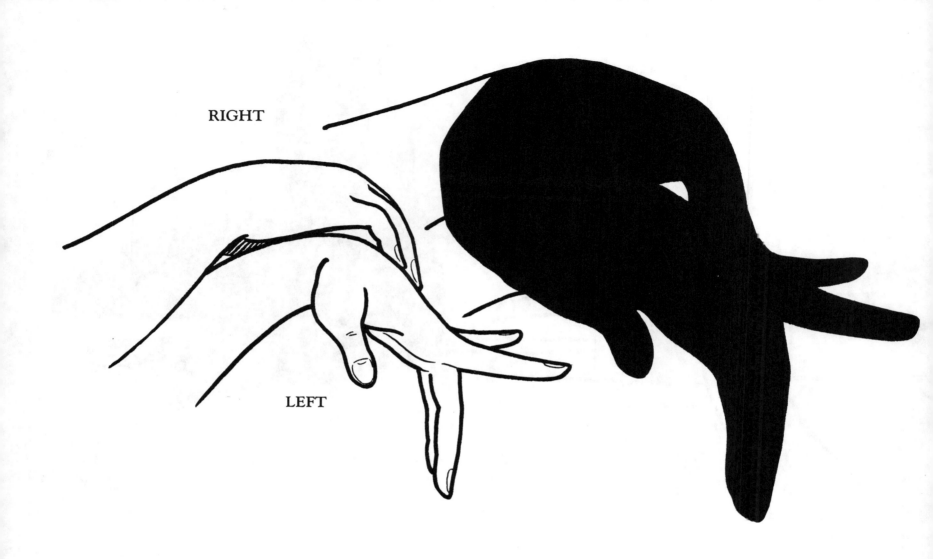

RIGHT

LEFT

## AN ELEPHANT

Here's an elephant, you can tell by his lengthy nose,
Comes of poking it in others' business, I suppose.
Let the elephant's long nose a lesson be to you—
Keep your nose at home or you may grow nosy looking too!

**Suggestions:** Have someone offer the elephant peanuts. With practice you will be able to carry a peanut with the two middle fingers of the left hand, which form the trunk, to the mouth.

LEFT

RIGHT

# A PANTHER

Here's a panther, fearful beast!
Cannot pet him in the least.
Panthers live in woods, and oh!
We are glad to have it so.

**Suggestions:** As the panther is such an exceedingly fierce creature, it is best to have him on the screen as short a time as possible. Open and shut his jaws a few times and let him vanish.

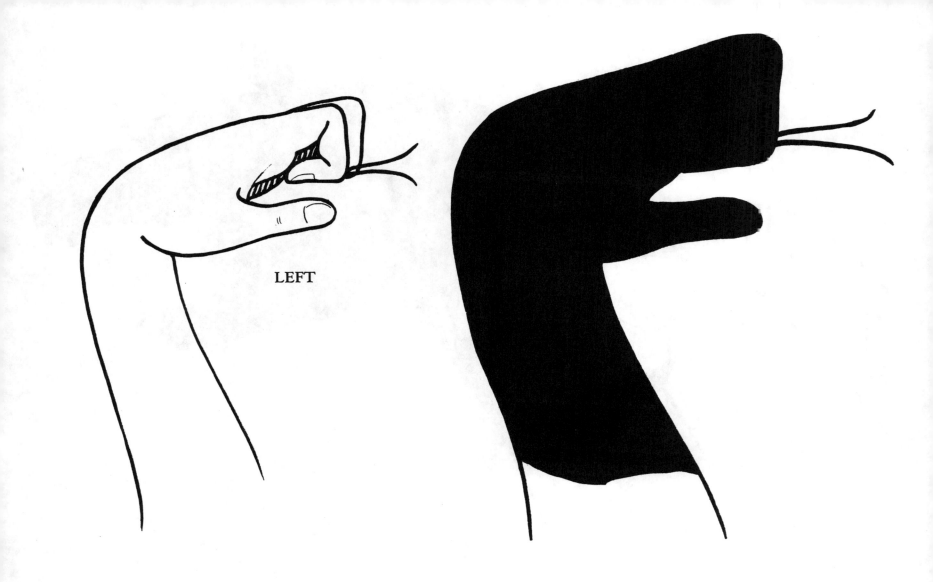

LEFT

# A SNAKE

This dreadful snake as black as night,
Is all prepared, I think to bite.
A snake will always lift his head
When he is angry, it is said.

**Suggestions:** Cut two very narrow strips of paper for fangs and hold them between the first and second fingers.

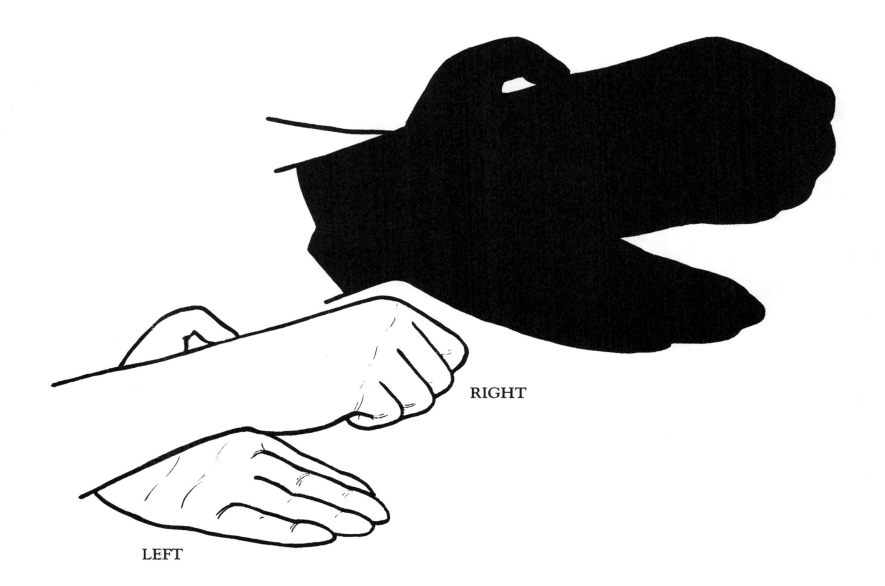

RIGHT

LEFT

# A HIPPOPOTAMUS

The hippo likes to take his ease
In squashy mud up to his knees.
One simply can't grow fond of him—
He has so little life and vim!

**Suggestions:** Move the two jaws together, very slowly, which is the way a hippopotamus does most things.

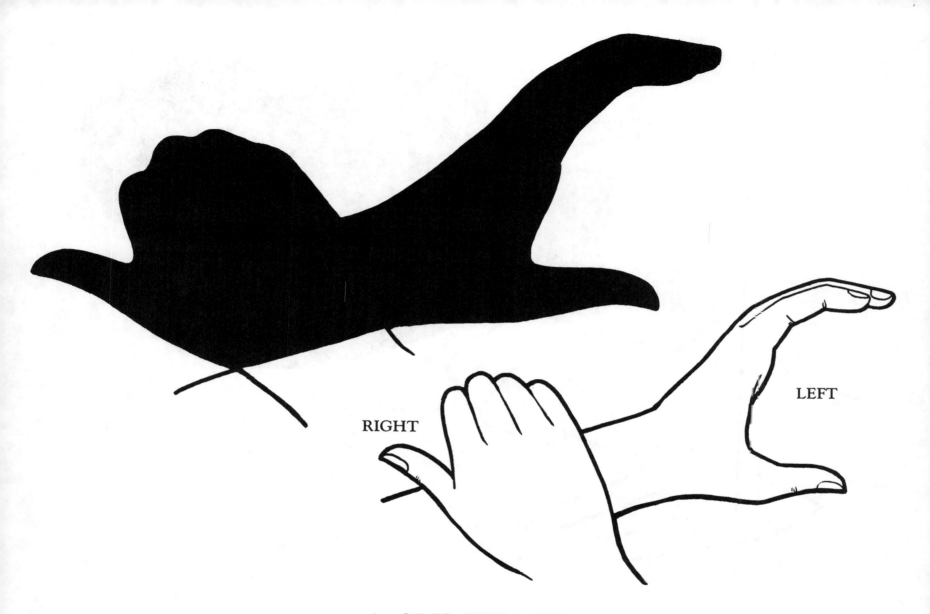

RIGHT

LEFT

# A SLY WEASEL

Here's a sly weasel, watch him creep
And suddenly he'll give a leap.
He hunts by night and sleeps by day
And sleepy chickens are his prey!

**Suggestions:** Move the hands, together, slowly across the screen, then tip them suddenly forward, as if the weasel had pounced upon some unsuspecting creature.

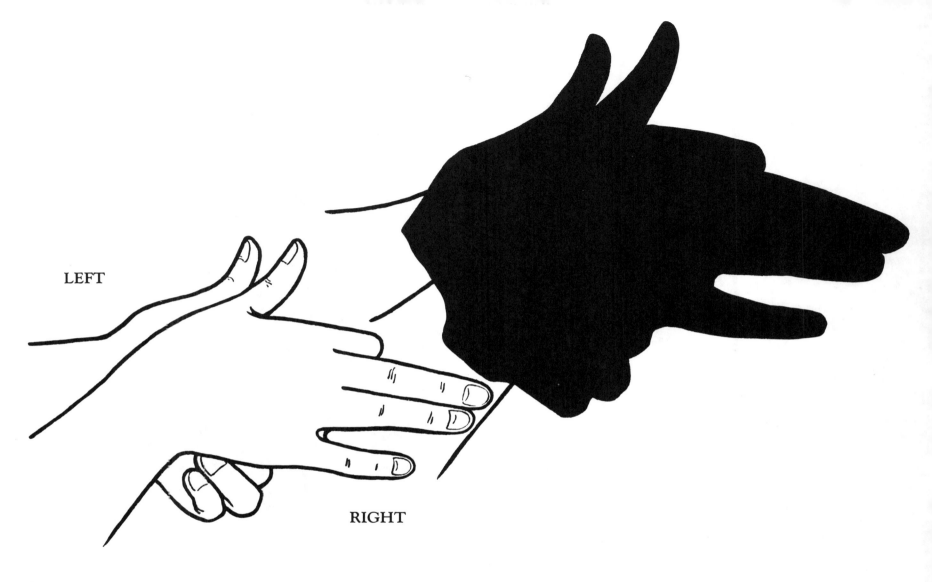

LEFT

RIGHT

## A DOG

Now here's a pet to suit the boys;
He has a bark that makes a noise!
He plays with children when it's light,
And keeps the thieves away at night.

**Suggestions:** Lower and raise first one thumb, then the other, as if the dog were pricking up his ears. You can also open and shut his mouth, and if you bark at the same time, it will make the shadow picture more lifelike.

RIGHT

LEFT

## A KANGAROO

This is, you see, a kangaroo;
What jumping stunts this beast can do!
In fact, he never has to run;
He jumps instead, and thinks it fun.

**Suggestions:** Tip the right hand forward and backward rapidly as you move both hands across the screen. The kangaroo will appear to be jumping.

LEFT

RIGHT

# A RABBIT

See this plump, pretty little rabbit,
He has a most engaging habit
Of wriggling both his lengthy ears,
Whenever some strange sound he hears!

**Suggestions:** The last three fingers on the left hand, that form the ears, can be easily wriggled, in imitation of a bunny. The rabbit can also be made to scratch his nose. Use the right forefinger, which forms one of his paws, for this trick.

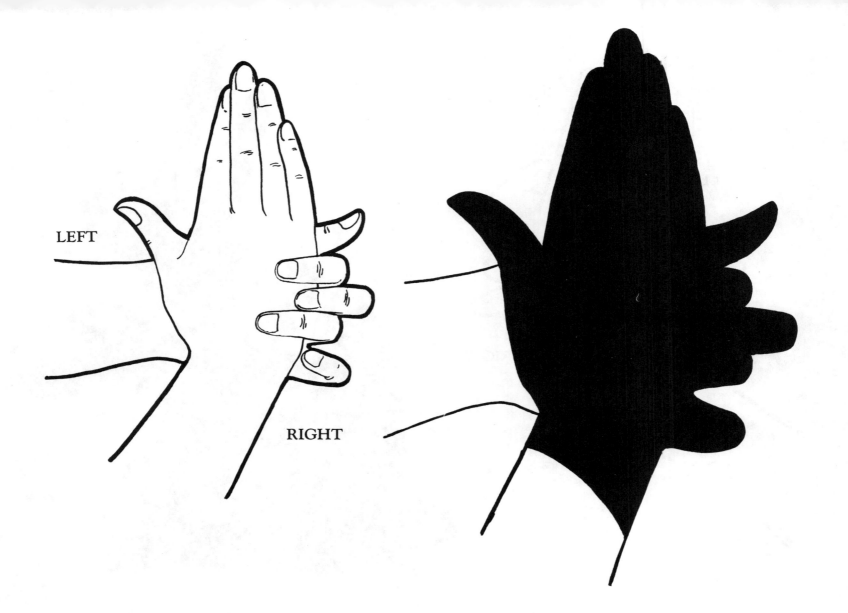

LEFT

RIGHT

## A CLOWN

This is the clown who ends the book;
He has a very merry look.
He's quite as good as all the rest,
And hopes, I think, you'll vote him best!

**Suggestions:** You can give the clown a dreadfully long nose by letting out the middle finger of your left hand, after you have it in position. Make the clown talk by wriggling upward the little finger on your left hand and say "Good-night" for him.